the cooking of provincial québec

MIRELLE BEAULIEU

GAGE PUBLISHING LIMITED • TORONTO

The illustrated recipes were prepared by
Les Filles du Roy restaurant and photographed
in their establishment in Vieux Montreal.

Cover and inside photographs: RENE DELBUGUET

First Published in French by
LES EDITIONS LA PRESSE, Montreal, Quebec

ISBN 0-7715-9942-0 Casebound
     0-7715-9943-9 Paperback

1 2 3 4 5 6 7 8 9   AP   80 79 78 77 76 75

INTRODUCTION

The most striking feature of traditional French-Canadian cooking is the extraordinary richness of the fare: eggs poached in maple syrup, three-crusted meat pies, hearth bread spread with savory pâté or drenched in cream. The habitants enjoyed a diet which would lead to heart failure for contemporary French Canadians who spend much of their time behind desks.

Although Quebec cooking has adjusted to the lighter calorie requirements of modern life, some specialties described in this book are more than 350 years old and can still be found prepared in the traditional way. These dishes owe their distinctiveness to the particular unfolding of events and conditions in early French Canada.

Nearly all of Quebec's earliest immigrants came from the west of France, a region producing an especially stout-hearted and energetic breed. They were of the working class (very few of the nobility emigrated to New France, even among the seigneurs), adventurers looking to Canada for a more stable and hopeful way of life than offered to them in their homeland.

The French government had, however, more sophisticated motives than the settlers. France at this time was in a mood of absolutism, fixed in its notions about social order and highly resistant to reform. With the failure of feudalism in Europe, France intended to graft the mercantile system onto the New World.

The immigrants were set to work clearing forests, building stockades, and cultivating the land as tenants under domination of the seigneurs — the incarnation of French authority. The seigneur extracted from the habitant a fixed portion of his yield, and the parish priest also insisted upon a large share. Locked into this rigid system, and ignorant of the fundamental principals of agriculture, the settlers could not prosper. Soil was soon exhausted, a situation that forced settlements to break ground further and further back from the banks of the St. Lawrence river.

For the habitant, it was a life of desperate hardship and stagnation — mitigated, finally, by the capitulation of Quebec to the English in 1759. This turn of events flipped French Canada from the frying pan into the fire. Under the less capricious English rule, she was able to establish herself as a viable agricultural society; but as a settlement of French-speaking Catholics in an English Canada, Quebec became an isolated enclave, abandoned by France, her mother country, for the next 200 years.

Not the least of these early trials was the harrowing experience of a Canadian winter. Probably no single factor has had more influence on French-Canadian habits. In the first years, many actually died from the paralyzing winter cold as well as from starvation and scurvy. To protect themselves from winter's assault, settlers began to build their houses on stone platforms about a foot wider than the base of the house itself. In winter, this foundation was covered with straw and tamped-down earth. It also became essential to line the interior of the house with wooden laths which were spread with plaster, or roughcast. Many of these eighteenth-century buildings still stand and the techniques have been handed down from generation to generation.

A typical Quebec house would be roughly 60 feet long and 20 feet wide, with cedar or pine rafters supporting the sloping roof. The whitewashed walls were interrupted by shuttered windows and dormers in the roof, and the houses had all the features of Normandy buildings. Settlers in this area were not as troubled by Iroquois raids as they were in Montreal, and their homesteads were more welcoming and exposed.

Around Montreal, the advance post to the east, Indians waged ceaseless war and the population was constantly on its guard. Every house in the Montreal district had to make a little fortress of itself. Square, massive, flanked by heavy chimneys, these houses were made of huge fieldstones, wedged with mortar. A few slits concealed behind thick shutters were cut into the walls, and the houses had a solitary, introverted aspect.

The Quebec winter also influenced the style of dress adapted by the French-Canadian settlers who took their cue from the Indians and wore loose, warm clothing made from animal skins and furs. Every household was equipped with a loom and spinning wheel for making hemp, linen, and wool cloth. Fine material was imported from France for townspeople who preferred to dress in style.

Again, it was the winter months which largely established the eating patterns of the habitants for the harsh climate demanded a rich diet that would sustain a workingman's energy. French Canadians became great meat eaters as game was plentiful — moose, caribou, venison, porcupine, and rabbit were staples of the meals. Ducks, pigeons, and partridge also abounded and the passenger pigeon was considered a special treat. It was killed by the hundreds of thousands and eaten freshly cooked through the summer months, then soaked in brine and smoked for winter storage. Fish also played an important part in the habitant's diet, with the St. Lawrence providing a mixture of freshwater and sea fish: salmon, haddock, sturgeon, bass, shad, and eel.

Gradually, as the soil was brought under cultivation, colonists were able to sow and harvest enough staples to keep from going hungry. Corn, oats, barley, peas, lentils, beans, and asparagus grew well. Some edibles were native to Canada and the first settlers came upon them growing wild; others, such as navy beans, potatoes, and sunflowers were brought over from Europe as seeds, and then germinated in Canadian soil.

Other vegetables gradually became part of the French-Canadian regime — cabbages, squash, shallots, leeks, carrots, and onions. Oddly enough, potatoes were not an especially popular food, for some time. Referred to disparagingly as "root," they were eaten only when things were desperate.

The household uses they found for potatoes were numerous, however. The residue squeezed from the grated pulp served as starch for the family laundry. Potatoes were used to soothe headaches and make yeast for bread; small pieces made good corks for bottles. Gradually they found their way into the stew pot, where their adaptability was apparently endless. Soon the potato was showing up at virtually every meal.

Maize was adopted from the Indians as the basic staple — easy to grow, nourishing for livestock, and useful in traditional recipes. It was eaten roasted over coals, mixed with game or fish, and mashed or ground into flour for bread. Mashed Indian corn, frozen and kept through the winter, formed the basis of the famous habitant pea soup. Corn flour was also used in a sort of pancake (less perishable than wheat or rye bread), or mixed with dried fish and peas and made into a soup known as "sagamite."

Many varieties of fruit grew wild, and abundantly: raspberries, strawberries, plums, blackberries, blueberries, cranberries, and apples. Preserving became a great art and all sorts of fruit compotes, jams, jellies, and relishes would fill the house with wonderful aromas as they simmered on the stone hearth every fall.

But fresh vegetables and fruits were a short-lived luxury, and French Canadians had to make the most of their brief growing season. As fall approached and the crops swelled, the produce was carefully gathered and prepared for storehouses where it would freeze, to be thawed and used over the long winter. Enormous quantities of game were also stockpiled in this way. Winter vegetables — turnips, carrots, beets, parsnips, cabbage, and onions — were also put in reserve to be used for soups and stews.

Great care was taken with the salting of pork, since this meat, with its tolerance for changes in temperature, formed the mainstay of Quebec cuisine. Salt bacon made a meal for farmers working in the heat of their summer fields, and it was indispensable to missionaries and coureurs de bois travelling in remote areas.

But there remained many items which were not available locally, and these had to be imported. Sweetmeats, nuts, citrus fruits, figs, olive oil, vinegar, and, originally, salt, sugar, spices, and molasses were luxuries for the consumption of only those who could afford them. Liquor was the biggest import. Brandy, rum, Spanish wines, and madiera were in heavy demand among the more affluent townspeople. Occasionally, rural dwellers would pool their money to buy a keg of rum, but the more practical alternative was to brew their own "bouillon" — a sort of beer made from a mash of wheat or maize, fermented, diluted with water, and allowed to mature in a cask.

The diet of rural and town dwellers naturally differed because of the higher caloric requirement of people working outdoors from dawn until dusk. Town folk ate three meals a day, beginning with breakfast which consisted of a light meal of bread or toast dipped in a mug of chocolate. Dinner at noon, and supper, the evening meal, were much alike; soup and bread were followed by a variety of fresh meat, game, or fowl served with several sorts of salad. The drink at dinner was usually claret, diluted with water. Dessert would be fruit, either raw or preserved — perhaps currants or cranberries crystallized in molasses, sweet jams, and walnuts, almonds and hazelnuts from France. Cheese also appeared with dessert, as well as milk taken with sugar.

In the countryside, peasants needed four full meals a day. They rose before dawn and put in three or four hours of labour before sitting down to breakfast at 8 o'clock. Breakfast and the evening meal were the heartiest of the day. Breakfast was usually pancakes made from wheat flour, well doused with maple syrup, and chunks of bread dipped in a bowl of creamy milk. Milk was nearly always served in preference to tea or coffee and country people drank quantities of it. The midday and 4 o'clock meals were considerably lighter, and eaten hurriedly. At the end of the day came a rich and leisurely meal of stews, meat pies, baked beans, or soup.

Periods of fasting, imposed by the Church, were strictly observed. No meat or milk by-products were eaten Fridays or during the 49 days of Lenten fast — 40 days of Lent and 9 days vigil for religious feast days. Bread, fish, and vegetables were the diet on these days when eating was restricted to one parsimonious meal usually taken at midday; this association with penance may account for the fact that French Canadians have never been enthusiastic fish eaters.

Cooking predispositions in French Canada have a mixed history. Jacques Cartier and the first settlers were from La Bretagne (Brittany) which, due to its proximity to England and because of the constant mingling of its seamen and fishermen with the English, was never as purely French in its eating habits as the rest of France. Foods favoured by the French Canadians such as beans, salt pork, peas, molasses, spices, puddings, and pies are of English origin. French influence on cooking in early Canada is felt mainly in the methods used to prepare food, rather than in the ingredients.

French cooking is also logical and precise; no step can be omitted and great care and pride is taken in preparing a dish in a certain way. English cooking is more approximate. It tends to be "pot cooking", making use of large pots, lots of water, vegetables, herbs, perhaps some wine, in quite a flexible way. It tends more to the "whatever's handy" style of cooking.

Many French-Canadian specialties point to this joint derivation. The famous cipaille, or six-pâtés, comes from the English "sea pie" and was originally a sort of coastal tourtière. Into the casserole, separated by thin layers of pastry, went every kind of seafood — haddock, cod, shad, bass, salmon, and sturgeon — seasoned with herbs and simmered in a covered dish for serveral hours. Eventually, cipaille came to refer to any dish similarly prepared, regardless of its ingredients.

Another renowned Canadian dish is the tourtière, traditionally eaten hot or cold after Midnight Mass on Christmas Eve. In France the tourtière was a special pie dish for cooking pigeon and other birds. The contents of the dish were known as "pièce toutière," and this phrase was carried over to New France. Over the years, however, the word "toutière" came to mean a pâté of fowl or game or very commonly, pork, prepared in the family stewpot and seasoned according to a special family recipe. It's often said that in Quebec there are as many tourtière recipes as there are cooks.

Pork has been the mainstay of French-Canadian cooking for over 300 years. Whether roasted, stewed, fried, ground, or eaten with beans or on bread as pâté, the Quebecois adore it. "Cretons", meat and herb flavoured fat renderings chilled in molds, are considered such delicacies that large companies make their own commercial brand and sell it in supermarkets.

But the crème de la crème in French Canada is maple sugar. The colonists developed a passion for it, and over the years countless maple sugar recipes have been invented . . . cakes, pies, maple creams, butters, fudge, wonderful desserts like "grand-pères au sirop" (maple syrup dumplings), not to mention the joy of pure maple syrup itself poured in a golden stream, over anything and everything.

Maple trees were the only source of sugar for many pioneer families, so each spring they stockpiled enough cakes of maple sugar to last the year. A sharp knife was used to shave off slivers of sugar to sprinkle on bread, desserts, or cereals; cakes were boiled down to syrup for a myriad of other uses.

The springtime flowing of the sap is still celebrated in Quebec. Tables are spread with a glorious feast of smoked ham, omelettes, potatoes, griddle cakes stuffed with bacon, cream, and french bread, and every heaped plate is lavishly annointed with maple syrup. This is also the season for "les toquettes" — warm sap threaded onto fresh snow to form a hard, clear taffy.

Certain regions of Quebec are renowned for particular specialties. The Lac St. Jean region in the north produces a very popular brown bean or lentil called the "gourgane", which is used fresh in summer and dried in winter. The "ouananiche", a delicate fresh-water salmon, also comes from this area, where the blueberries — "the blue pearls of the Saguenay" — are also especially delicious.

Other traditional dishes are best known by the cooking implement used in their preparation. The "pot au feu," a black iron kettle with a good lid, was part of every girl's dowry; this was used for the long, slow simmering of soup or stew, or for special pies. Meat simmered in a liquid with lots of fragrant root vegetables was the true "pot au feu." This was served with big slices of homemade oven bread, toasted on the wood stove. A slice of bread was placed in the bottom of a large deep soup plate, then bouillon from the "pot au feu" was poured on top until it was soaked up by the bread; the bread was then topped with pieces of meat and vegetables. A black iron frying pan for meatloaf and sausages, and plenty of earthenware pudding dishes were essential to a habitant kitchen as well.

Bread was baked in a distinctly French-Canadian way. To work the dough before baking, an implement called a mixer was used — a large pail with a curved rod inside and a crank on the top. The ingredients were thrown in and the crank rotated for twenty minutes. Special outdoor ovens, shaped like a beehive or half an eggshell, were used for baking. A hot fire was made in this clay and stone structure; then the ashes were swept out, the stone hearth sprinkled with cornmeal, and the bread was baked on the hearthstone. (Bread made this way is still sold to tourists driving along the banks of the St. Lawrence.)

The interior of a habitant house must have been a cheerful, bustling scene with its one large room amply serving as kitchen, livingroom, and bedroom. At the huge chimneypiece with its open fire and flagstone hearth, there were hooks for pots and pans, a shovel for the ashes, a great cauldron and stockpots, stew pans, dripping pans, pie dishes, a gridiron, a demi-john — an army of utensils. On a ledge hung a set of flatirons, a tin lamp, and some candlesticks.

The master bed was the other main fixture in the room. It was huge, hung with a canopy almost six feet high. The children's beds were ranged in the shadow of this enormous piece of furniture. The rest of the house contained rudimentary furnishings — five or six wooden chairs with rush seats, a spinning wheel and spindle, a loom, a trough, a table to seat upwards of twelve, two or three coffers, a wardrobe, and a water carrier next to the door.

The hearth was the heart of habitant life. Here food for both family and animals was prepared, clothes were warmed, work tools were placed to thaw out. Here travellers and neighbours were welcomed. Hospitality is an old and deep tradition with French Canadians. In the early days, settler life offered no form of recreation. The church discouraged social life of any kind as impious, and there was no theatre, no concert hall, no library, and no market place. Sunday worship was a solemn occasion, not an opportunity to mix and mingle. As a result, social gatherings took place in one another's homes.

Friendly visiting was facilitated by the characteristic way in which farms were laid out in long narrow strips extending away from the river, so that houses were close together. Neighbours had cause for powerful solidarity; the common difficulties they faced gave rise to a cohesiveness that is still in evidence today.

It was in the fields and in each others homes that Quebec folksongs, legends, and folklore began. The deep spirituality of the settlers and their reverence for the past gave rise to wonderful hunting tales, ghost stories, and accounts of religious visions received by the people. On many an evening, the family and friends would be gathered around the hearth, mother at her spinning wheel in the firelight, grandfather in his chair and the children huddled closely around the storyteller.

If habitant life was hard, it was also a full life and a rich one, producing a culinary legacy appreciated over generations and still cherished all over French Canada. It is hoped that the recipes in this book will impart some of the pleasure of French-Canadian life to all who try them.

Contents

the cooking of provincial québec

Homemade Vegetable Soup and French-Canadian Pea Soup

Potted Pork and Head Cheese

Hor-d'oeuvres

1 lb. ground pork
1 cup breadcrumbs
1 grated onion
½ tsp. salt
⅛ tsp. pepper
1 garlic clove, crushed
¼ tsp. cinnamon
¼ tsp. nutmeg
1 cup milk

Potted Pork

Cretons

Put all ingredients in a saucepan and mix well. Cover and simmer on low heat for an hour, stirring occasionally.

Turn into a mold and refrigerate. *Serves 6-8.*

½ lb. chicken, pork,
    beef, or calf's liver,
    cut in pieces
½ lb. pork fat, diced
¾ cup cold water
2 cloves garlic
1 onion, chopped
1 bay leaf
1 pinch of thyme
1 pinch of savory
½ tsp. salt
¼ tsp. pepper

Foie Gras

Put all ingredients in a saucepan and bring to a boil. Simmer over low heat for half an hour. Leave to cool.

Liquefy in blender and turn into a mold; cover and refrigerate. *Serves 6-8.*

3-4 lbs. pork shoulder
3 cups water
1 tsp. salt
½ tsp. pepper
1 large onion, chopped
1 clove garlic, crushed
1 bay leaf
1 tsp. savory
¼ tsp. ground cloves

Pork Galantine

Galantine de porc

Wipe the meat with a damp towel. Melt a little pork fat in a heavy skillet and brown the pork shoulder on all sides. When the meat is well-browned, add all the other ingredients and simmer over low heat for 2 to 2½ hours.

Remove the meat, bone it, and cut into small pieces. Place the pieces of meat in a mold that has been rinsed in cold water and put to one side.

Put all the bones in a saucepan, cover with water and boil them on high heat for 20 minutes. Pour the stock over the meat, filling the mold. Cover and refrigerate until the jelly is firm. *Serves 8-10.*

1 5-6 lb. chicken
8 cups hot water
1 tsp. salt
½ tsp. pepper
1 grated carrot
1 cup diced celery
1 bay leaf
1 tsp. savory
1 onion, minced

Chicken Galantine

Galantine de poulet

Melt a little fat from the chicken in a large saucepan and brown the chicken on all sides.

Add all the other ingredients and bring to a boil. Cover and simmer over low heat for 2 to 3 hours or until the chicken is tender.

Remove the chicken and boil off half the stock over high heat.

Bone the chicken and cut the meat into small pieces; place the meat in a greased mold, pour the stock over it, cover, and refrigerate for at least 12 hours. *Serves 8-10*.

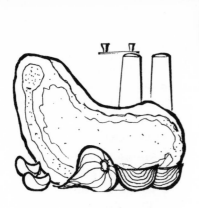

5 lbs. pork loin
2 cloves garlic, coarsely
  chopped
2 onions, quartered
¼ tsp. savory
1 tsp. salt
½ tsp. pepper

Pork Pâté
(from Drippings)

Graisse de rôti

Make a number of incisions in the roast and insert the garlic pieces. Remove a little of the fat and melt it in a heavy skillet.

Brown the meat on all sides in the fat; add the onions, savory, salt, and pepper. Simmer over low heat.

When the roast is cooked through, remove it from the skillet and pour in 1½ to 2 cups of cold water. Boil for 10 minutes, scraping the bottom of the skillet thoroughly. Pour the liquid into individual serving dishes and chill until firm. *Serves 8-10*.

1 pig's head
1 pig's hock
2 cloves garlic
1 large onion, quartered
2 carrots
1 bay leaf
6 sprigs of celery tops
4 sprigs of parsley
3 whole cloves
1 tbsp. carroway seeds
12 peppercorns
¼ tsp. thyme
salt

Head Cheese

Tête fromagée

Have the butcher remove the eyes and snout from the pig's head. Scrub thoroughly and place the pieces in a large kettle. The brain should be removed and added 20 minutes before the meat is done.

Tie up in a cheesecloth bag the following ingredients: chopped onion, celery tops, parsley, carrots, garlic, cloves, bay leaf, and 12 peppercorns. Place the cheesecloth bag in the kettle with the meat and cover with water. Add ¼ tsp. thyme and salt to taste.

Bring the mixture slowly to a boil, skim, and reduce the heat. Simmer gently for 4 hours or until the meat falls from the bones. Remove the meat from the broth, discard the cheesecloth bag and strain the broth into a clean kettle, reserving all pieces of meat which may have fallen from the bones. Boil the broth uncovered until it reduces to about 3 cups.

Remove the meat from the bones, being careful to pick out the small splinters. Cut the meat, skin, and fat into small pieces with a pair of scissors. Put the cut-up pieces into the reduced broth, add 1 tbsp. carraway seeds, and simmer for about 10 minutes. Taste for seasoning and pour into molds. Cool and chill.

Soups

3 lbs. beef shank
10 cups water
1 large onion, chopped
1 bay leaf
1 tbsp. salt
¼ tsp. pepper
4 cups grated cabbage
1½ cups chopped leeks
2 cups diced celery
1 cup grated carrots

Cabbage Soup

Soupe au chou

Pour the water into a large pot and bring to a boil. Add the beef shank, onion, bay leaf, salt, and pepper. Simmer over low heat for 2 to 2½ hours, or until the beef is quite tender.

Then add the cabbage, leeks, and celery, and continue cooking for 30 minutes. Ten minutes before the cooking time is up, add the grated carrots. *Serves 6.*

3 lbs. either halibut,
  haddock, or cod
2 cups diced potatoes
1 large onion, chopped
2 celery stalks, finely
  chopped
1 bay leaf
2 tsp. salt
¼ tsp. pepper
2 tbsp. flour
2 tbsp. butter or margarine
1 qt. milk
fresh parsley

Fish Soup

Soupe au poisson

Cut the fish into bite-sized pieces and place in a large soup kettle with the following six ingredients. Add water to cover and boil for 20 minutes.

Melt the butter in another pot; stir in the flour; pour in the milk and cook, stirring constantly, until thick.

Add this sauce to the fish and other ingredients and garnish with the fresh parsley. *Serves 6-8*.

2 cups navy beans
3 tbsp. mixed herbs
1 lb. side bacon, cut into
  pieces
1 cup carrots, finely diced
1 chopped onion
¼ cup barley
3 qts. cold water
2 tsp. salt
½ tsp. pepper

Bean Soup

Soupe aux gourganes

Soak beans overnight. Strain, reserving liquid. Add enough cold water to liquid to equal 3 quarts. Put all ingredients in a large kettle or saucepan and bring to a boil.

Simmer over low heat for 2½ to 3 hours. Serve hot. *Serves 6.*

2 lbs. beef shank
1 bay leaf
1 whole clove
¼ tsp. marjoram
1 tsp. salt
¼ tsp. pepper
1 can tomatoes (20 oz.)
1 tbsp. sugar
2 onions, chopped
1 cup diced carrots
½ cup diced turnip
1 cup diced celery

Vegetable Soup

Soupe aux légumes

Put the beef in a large saucepan with the bay leaf, clove, marjoram, salt, pepper, tomatoes, and sugar. Add cold water to cover and bring to a boil. Cover the saucepan and simmer for 2 hours, skimming frequently.

Add all the vegetables and continue cooking for 30 minutes or until the vegetables are tender. *Serves 4-6.*

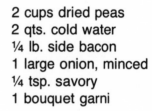

2 cups dried peas
2 qts. cold water
¼ lb. side bacon
1 large onion, minced
¼ tsp. savory
1 bouquet garni

Pea Soup

Soupe aux pois

Wash the peas and soak them overnight in a quart of cold water. Once you are ready to begin cooking, add the second quart of cold water, the bacon, onion, savory, and bouquet garni.

Simmer over low heat for 3 hours. *Serves 4.*

3 or 4 green tomatoes,
  chopped
1 minced onion
½ tsp. salt
¼ tsp. pepper
¼ tsp. cinnamon
½ tsp. sugar
1 tsp. baking soda
2 cups water
4 tbsp. butter or margarine
4 tbsp. flour
1 qt. milk

Green Tomato Soup

Soupe aux tomates vertes

Put the tomatoes in a saucepan along with the onion, salt, pepper, cinnamon, sugar, and water. Boil for 10 to 15 minutes. Add the baking soda.

Melt the butter in a second saucepan; blend in the flour; pour in the milk and cook, stirring constantly, until the sauce is creamy. Add the tomato mixture, stirring thoroughly, and serve immediately. *Serves 4.*

Meat Pie and Stewed Pig's Feet

Cipâte

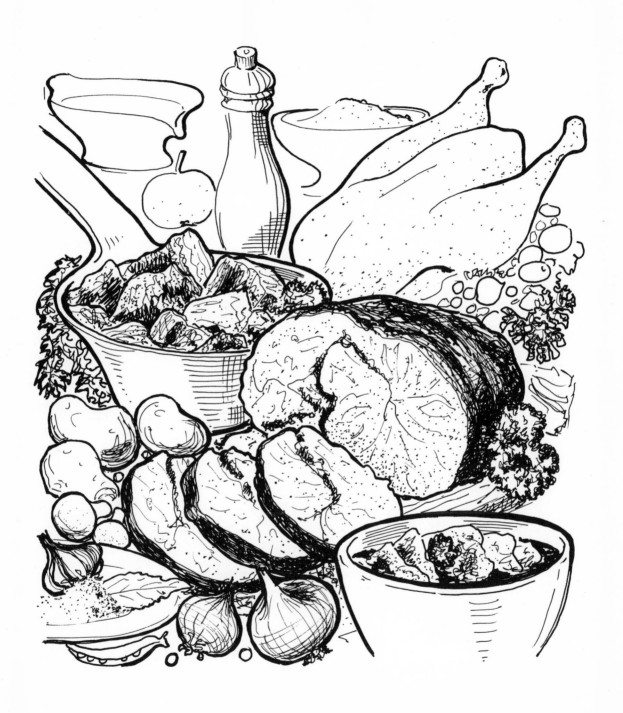

Meat Dishes

3-4 lbs. lamb shoulder
4 tbsp. flour
4-5 tbsp. butter or margarine
2 carrots, sliced in rounds
1 large onion, minced
2 celery stalks, cut in pieces
12 sprigs fresh parsley
¼ tsp. thyme
1 bay leaf
3 cups hot water
salt & pepper
1 can of green peas, drained.

Lamb Stew with Green Peas

Ragoût d'agneau aux petits pois

Cut the meat into 1-inch cubes. Dredge with flour, and brown in melted butter or margarine. Remove meat; add any remaining flour and let it brown.

Pour in hot water and add all the other ingredients except the peas. Cover and simmer over low heat for 1½ hours.

Add the peas 5 minutes before the stew is ready. *Serves 4-6*.

4 lbs. top round beef, cut
 in cubes
3-4 tbsp. chopped salt pork
boiling water
1 tsp. salt
⅛ tsp. pepper
a pinch of thyme
1 bay leaf
1 sprig fresh parsley
a few carrots and small
 onions

Beef A La Mode

Boeuf a la mode

Melt the salt pork in a heat-proof casserole and brown the cubes of beef on all sides. Pour off excess fat and add boiling water to cover; cover the casserole and cook for 15 to 20 minutes.

Add the salt, pepper, thyme, bay leaf, and parsley. Cover again and continue cooking over low heat for 2 hours.

Slice carrots and glaze onions in a little butter and sugar; add to casserole and cook until tender. *Serves 8-10*.

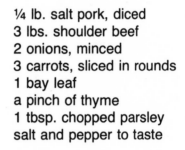

¼ lb. salt pork, diced
3 lbs. shoulder beef
2 onions, minced
3 carrots, sliced in rounds
1 bay leaf
a pinch of thyme
1 tbsp. chopped parsley
salt and pepper to taste

Braised Beef

Boeuf braisé

Brown the salt pork in a heavy skillet; add the meat and brown on all sides.

Add the onions, carrots, bay leaf, thyme, parsley, and enough boiling water to cover the bottom of the skillet. Cover and simmer over low heat for 2 hours or until the meat is tender.

Add salt and pepper after it has cooked for half an hour. *Serves 5-6*.

3 lbs. beef brisket
1 lb. side bacon
2 qts. cold water
1 tsp. salt
¼ tsp. pepper
1 bay leaf
½ tsp. savory
1 small cabbage, quartered
1 small turnip, quartered
5 celery sticks, cut in 2
3 onions, cut in 2
6 potatoes
½ lb. wax beans
½ lb. green beans
6 to 8 carrots
6 ears corn

Pot Roast

Le bouilli

Put the beef and the bacon in a large kettle or saucepan. Add the water, salt, pepper, bay leaf, and savory. Simmer over low heat for 2 to 2½ hours.

Add all the vegetables and continue cooking for about 30 minutes until the vegetables are tender. *Serves 6-8*.

2 tbsp. butter or margarine
1 cup chopped onion
3 cups diced raw potato
¼ tsp. savory
salt & pepper
2 cups cooked meat, cut into
  small pieces
juices from roast
salt and pepper to taste

Fricassee

La fricassée

Brown the onion in the butter. Add the potatoes, savory, salt, pepper, meat, meat juices, and cold water to cover.

Cover the pot and cook on low heat for 30 minutes, stirring gently from time to time. Serve hot. *Serves 3-4.*

3-4 tbsp. butter or margarine
2 diced onions
2 cups chopped cooked
  meat (or 1 lb. hamburger)
¼ tsp. savory
salt & pepper to taste
2 cups creamed corn
mashed potatoes

Shepherd's Pie

Pâté chinois

Preheat the oven to 375°.

Melt butter in a skillet and brown the onions. Add the meat, savory, salt, and pepper. Cook for 4 or 5 minutes.

Turn this mixture into a greased baking dish. Cover the meat with creamed corn and top it all off with the mashed potatoes. Dot with knobs of butter, and brown in the oven. *Serves 3-4.*

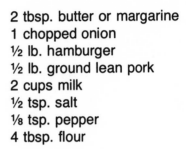

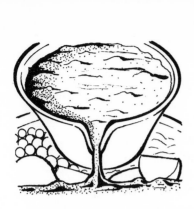

2 tbsp. butter or margarine
1 chopped onion
½ lb. hamburger
½ lb. ground lean pork
2 cups milk
½ tsp. salt
⅛ tsp. pepper
4 tbsp. flour

Meat Sauce

Sauce à la viande

Melt butter in a large skillet and brown the onion and meat for 4 or 5 minutes.

Pour in the milk, add salt and pepper, and bring to a boil over medium heat. Thicken the sauce by adding the flour mixed with a little cold water.

Cook, stirring frequently, until the sauce reaches the desired consistency. *Serves 3-4*.

2 tbsp. flour
1 tsp. salt
¼ tsp. pepper
2 lbs. beef (brisket or
   shoulder), cut in pieces
2 tbsp. fat
1¾ cups hot water
1 tsp. Worcestershire sauce
¼ tsp. rosemary
4 small whole onions
4 to 6 carrots, cut into
   pieces
1 cup diced celery

Beef Stew with Dumplings

Ragoût de boeuf avec grands-pères

Dredge the beef in a mixture of flour, salt, and pepper.

Melt the fat in a large saucepan; add meat and brown. Add hot water, Worcestershire sauce, rosemary, and onions. Cover and simmer for 2 to 2½ hours, or until the meat is tender. Stir occasionally.

Add the vegetables and continue cooking for another 20 minutes. *Serves 4-5.*

1½ cups flour
2 tsp. baking powder
a pinch of salt
¼ cup lard
1 tbsp. chopped parsley
1 egg
½ cup milk

The Dumplings
Grands-pères

Combine flour, baking powder, and salt. Cut the lard into small pieces and add to the mixture, along with parsley, milk and egg beaten up together. Mix rapidly and drop by spoonfuls into the stew.

Cook for 20 minutes. (To keep the dumplings light, leave the pot covered during cooking.)

4 pork chops, 1 inch thick
1 clove garlic, cut into
   pieces
4 medium potatoes, sliced
2 onions, sliced
1½ cups sour cream
½ tsp. dry mustard
salt & pepper to taste

Oven-baked Pork Chops

Côtelletes de porc au four

Preheat the oven to 350°.

Trim a little of the fat from the pork chops and melt in a frying pan. Dredge meat in flour and brown with the garlic. Add salt and pepper.

Grease a baking dish thoroughly. Arrange potato slices at the bottom of the dish and place pork chops and slices of onion on top.

Mix the sour cream with mustard and pour over chops. Bake for 2 hours or until the chops are tender. *Serves 4.*

4 cups dried beans
1 cup salt pork, sliced
1 large onion, minced
2 tbsp. dry mustard
¾ cup molasses

Baked Beans

Fèves au lard

Soak the beans in cold water for 12 hours. Bring to a boil and continue boiling for half an hour.

Pour the beans and water into an earthenware container (if one is available). Then add salt pork, onion, mustard, molasses, and hot water to cover.

Cover the container and put in a 375° oven to bake for 4 to 6 hours. Add extra hot water during cooking to keep beans moist.

To brown, remove cover from the container during the last half hour of cooking. *Serves 6.*

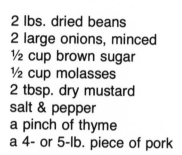

2 lbs. dried beans
2 large onions, minced
½ cup brown sugar
½ cup molasses
2 tbsp. dry mustard
salt & pepper
a pinch of thyme
a 4- or 5-lb. piece of pork

Baked Beans with Meatballs

Fèves au lard garnies

Soak the beans overnight in enough cold water to cover.

The next morning, put beans and water in a large pot, adding additional cold water, if necessary, to cover the beans completely. Add all the other ingredients and bake at 225° for 8 hours. *Serves 10-12.*

The Meatballs

1½ lbs. hamburger
2/3 cup milk
1 egg
½ cup cracker crumbs
½ cup minced onion
1 tsp. garlic salt
1 tbsp. prepared mustard
½ tsp. salt
2 tbsp. vegetable shortening

The Sauce

1½ cups ketchup
3 tbsp. vinegar
3 tbsp. brown sugar
¾ tsp. dry mustard
1 tbsp. Worcestershire sauce

Prepare the meatballs by mixing together all the ingredients except the vegetable shortening. Brown meatballs on all sides in the melted shortening and put them to one side.

To make the sauce, put all ingredients in the pan where the meatballs have cooked and mix well. Heat and stir until brown sugar is dissolved; add meatballs and keep warm.

Half an hour before the beans finish cooking, add meatballs. Cook until meatballs and beans are tender. Serve hot.

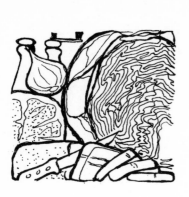

4 slices salt pork
5 lbs. pork fillet
1 clove garlic, cut into
  pieces
1 small cabbage, chopped
1 large onion, sliced
1 tsp. salt
½ tsp. pepper

Fillet of Pork with Cabbage

Filet de porc au chou

Make a number of small incisions in meat and insert garlic pieces.

Melt salt pork in a large, preferably thick-bottomed skillet. Add meat and cook until brown on all sides.

Add cabbage, onion, salt, and pepper. Cover and cook over medium heat until pork is tender. It may be necessary to add a little water during cooking to keep the meat from sticking to the bottom of the pan. *Serves 8*.

Pot Roast and Lamb Stew with Peas

Roast Duck

1 5-6 lb. ham
4 cups cold water
4 cups beer
2 medium onions
1 bay leaf
1 cup molasses
1 carrot and 1 celery stick
1 tsp. salt
¼ tsp. pepper
whole cloves

The Glaze

½ cup brown sugar
½ cup breadcrumbs
1 tbsp. dry mustard
cold water

Ham with Beer

Jambon à la bière

Put ham in a large kettle and add all other ingredients, except the whole cloves. Cook over low heat for 4 to 4½ hours. Let ham cool without removing from the liquid.

When cool, remove ham from the kettle and peel off the skin. Make diamond-shaped incisions in the fat and place a clove in each one. Place ham in a large broiling pan, with the fatty part up, and pour the glaze over it.

Cook in a preheated 400° oven for 25 to 30 minutes.

To prepare glaze, mix all the ingredients with just enough cold water to make it spread easily. *Serves 10-12.*

8 cups apple juice
1½ cups raisins
cold water
1 5-6 lb. ham
whole cloves
2 cups maple sugar
¼ tsp. dry mustard

Ham with Maple Sugar

Jambon de la cabane à sucre

Pour apple juice into a large kettle and bring to a rolling boil. Place ham in the juice, cover, and simmer over low heat for 2 to 2½ hours, or until ham is cooked.

Meanwhile, put raisins into a smaller saucepan and add enough cold water to cover. Simmer over low heat until tender.

When ham is cooked, take from the juice, remove the skin, make diamond-shaped incisions in the fat, and place a clove in each one.

Mix maple sugar with mustard and add just enough cold water to make a thick paste. Spread paste over the ham. Place ham in a large broiling pan and pour raisin sauce over it.
Preheat oven to 300° and bake ham for 30 minutes.

If the sauce is too thin, thicken with a little flour and water.
Serves 10-12.

1 5-lb. ham
½ cup milk
1 large onion, pierced with
  a few cloves
2 carrots
1 bay leaf
2 oz. apple jelly
⅓ cup of maple syrup

Glazed Ham

Jambon glacé

Place the ham in a large kettle and add enough cold water to cover. Add milk, onion studded with cloves, carrots, and bay leaf. Bring to a boil and simmer over low heat for 2 to 3 hours. Let ham cool in the liquid.

Remove the ham from the liquid, peel off skin and place the ham in a large broiling pan.

Add apple jelly to maple syrup in a small pot and boil for 4 minutes. Spread sauce on ham and bake at 350° for 1 hour. Baste with additional sauce from time to time as it cooks. *Serves 8-10*.

4 lbs. pork loin
1 4-5 lb. chicken
2 cloves garlic, cut into
   pieces
   salt and pepper
1 large onion, sliced
1 or 2 carrots, cut in
   rounds
1 sprig of fresh parsley
a few bay leaves
1 cup chicken stock

Braised Chicken and Pork

Porc et poule braisés

Remove a little fat from the chicken and melt it in a large heat-proof casserole. Make a number of small incisions in the pork roast and insert the pieces of garlic.

Brown pork and chicken in hot fat. Add salt and pepper and the rest of the ingredients. Cover and cook in the oven at 350° for 2½ hours.

Remove cover from the casserole and continue cooking until meat is tender. Add a little extra stock if necessary to keep the meat moist. *Serves 10-15.*

2 lbs. lean, ground pork
¼ tsp. ground cloves
1 chopped onion
¼ tsp. cinnamon
¼ tsp. dry mustard
salt & pepper
4-5 tbsp. butter or margarine
4 cups boiling water
¼ to ½ cup browned flour

Meatball Stew

Ragoût de boulettes

Mix the first 6 ingredients thoroughly, form mixture into balls, and dust lightly with flour.

Melt the butter or margarine in a skillet and brown the meatballs. Once they are well browned, pour in boiling water. Cover skillet and simmer over low heat for 1 hour.

Put flour in a frypan and stir constantly over medium heat until golden. Thicken the sauce by gradually adding the browned flour mixed with cold water. *Serves 5-6*.

4 pig's feet
all-purpose flour
salt & pepper to taste
½ tsp. cinnamon
¼ tsp. ground cloves
a pinch of nutmeg
4 tbsp. butter or margarine
2 or 3 onions
6-8 tbsp. browned flour

Stewed Pig's Feet

Ragoût de pattes de porc

Wash and dry pig's feet thoroughly and cut in half.

Mix a little flour with salt, pepper, cinnamon, cloves, and nutmeg, and roll the pig's feet in this mixture. Brown on all sides in butter or margarine.

Add onions, and enough water to cover. Simmer over low heat for 2 to 3 hours, or until meat is tender. Put flour in a frypan and stir constantly over medium heat until golden.

Thicken the sauce by adding the browned flour mixed with a little cold water.

Serve with boiled potatoes. *Serves 4-6*.

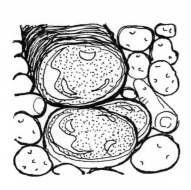

5 lbs. pork loin or shoulder
2 cloves garlic, cut into
  pieces
1 tsp. salt
½ tsp. pepper
¼ tsp. savory
2 onions, quartered
¼ cup water
potatoes
carrots

Roast of Pork with Garlic

Rôti de porc à l'ail

Make a number of incisions in the roast and insert pieces of garlic.

Remove a few pieces of fat from meat and melt them in a cast-iron skillet. Brown roast on all sides in the fat.

Add all other ingredients except potatoes and carrots. Cover and simmer over low heat for 2 to 3 hours, or until meat is tender. Turn the roast from time to time as it cooks and add more water to keep it from sticking to the bottom, if necessary.

An hour before cooking time is up, add a few potatoes and carrots. *Serves 4-6*.

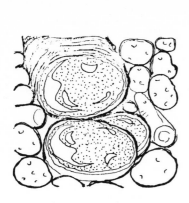

5 lbs. pork loin, skin on
2 cloves garlic, chopped
1 tsp. salt
¼ tsp. pepper
1 tsp. savory
1 tsp. dry mustard
2 cups water
a few small potatoes

Roast of Pork with Baked Potatoes

Rôti de porc aux patates brunes

Preheat the oven to 325°.

Remove the skin from the meat and place roast on the skin, fatty side down in a heat-proof casserole.

Make a number of incisions in the meat and insert garlic pieces. Add salt, pepper, savory, dry mustard, and water. Cook in the oven for 2 hours, basting frequently.

During the final hour of cooking, add the potatoes and a little water to keep the roast moist. *Serves 6.*

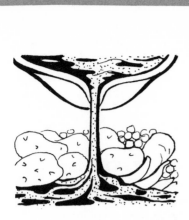

1-2 tbsp. butter or margarine
1 large onion, chopped
3-4 tbsp. flour
2 cups milk
1 lb. sausage meat or
  skinless sausage
salt & pepper to taste

Sausage Gravy

Sauce au boudin

Divide the sausage into 2 portions: mash the first portion thoroughly with a fork, and cut the second portion into large chunks. Put to one side.

Brown onion in the butter or margarine, sprinkle in the flour and blend thoroughly. Pour in milk and cook for about 8 to 10 minutes.

Add sausage, salt, and pepper. Cook until sausage is tender. *Serves 4-6.*

3-4 kidneys, depending
  on size
2 tbsp. vegetable shortening
2 tbsp. butter or margarine
1 onion, chopped
2 cups boiling water
¼ cup Madeira (optional)
salt & pepper
4 tbsp. browned flour

Kidney Gravy

Sauce aux rognons

Remove fat and thin membrane covering the kidneys. Cut in half, lengthwise, and remove white part from inside, then cut into cubes.

Melt shortening and butter in a heavy skillet and brown kidneys and onion. When kidneys are done, add boiling water, Madeira, salt, and pepper. Cover and simmer over low heat until kidneys are tender.

After the kidneys are cooked through, brown the flour by stirring in a frypan over medium heat until golden. Thicken the sauce by adding the browned flour mixed with a little cold water.

Continue cooking until the sauce thickens. *Serves 4-6.*

1 lb. lean, ground pork
1 medium onion, chopped
salt & pepper
¼ tsp. savory
¼ tsp. ground cloves
1 bay leaf
¼ cup boiling water
short pastry for 2 crusts

Meat Pie

Tourtière

Put first 7 ingredients in a saucepan and mix well. Add boiling water and simmer uncovered for 20 minutes, stirring occasionally.

Remove bay leaf and skim off any fat.

Roll out half the pastry and line a 9-inch pie plate. Place filling in pie plate and cover with the remaining pastry. Make an incision in the centre to allow steam to escape.

Bake in a preheated 375° oven for 30 minutes, or until the crust is golden. Serve hot. *Serves 4-5.*

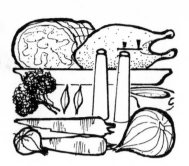

1 5-6 lb. chicken
5-6 tbsp. butter or margarine
cold water
salt & pepper
1 large onion, minced
½ tsp. poultry seasoning
1 lb. lean, ground pork
1 large onion, finely chopped
1 clove garlic, crushed
¼ tsp. savory
¼ tsp. marjoram
1 egg, beaten
1 tsp. salt
½ tsp. pepper
all-purpose flour

Chicken Stew with Meatballs

Ragoût de poule aux boulettes

Cut chicken into several pieces and brown on all sides in the butter or margarine, in a heavy skillet.

Then add enough cold water to fill the skillet to about the ⅓ mark. Add salt, pepper, onion, and poultry spice. Bring to a boil, simmer over low heat for 1½ to 2 hours or until chicken is tender.

Meanwhile, prepare the meatballs by mixing the pork with the onion, garlic, savory, marjoram, egg, salt, and pepper. Shape mixture into small balls and dust them lightly with flour.

After the chicken pieces are cooked, remove from the skillet and bring the stock to a rolling boil. Put meatballs in the stock and cook for 4 or 5 minutes, stirring gently.

Bone chicken pieces and return them to the stock.

If sauce is too thin, thicken by adding a little flour mixed with cold water. *Serves 8-10*.

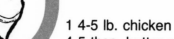

1 4-5 lb. chicken
4-5 tbsp. butter or margarine
8 cups hot water
1 tsp. salt
¼ tsp. pepper
1 carrot, sliced
1 large onion, minced
1 clove
1 bay leaf
a pinch of thyme
1 clove garlic, crushed

The Dumplings

2 cups all-purpose flour
4 tsp. baking powder
salt
2 eggs
1 cup milk

Chicken Stew with Dumplings

Ragoût de poule avec grands-pères

Cut chicken into pieces and brown on all sides in the butter or margarine. Add all other ingredients and bring to a boil. Cover the saucepan and simmer over low heat for 1½ to 2 hours, or until the chicken is tender.

Next prepare the dumplings. Beat eggs with the milk. Add the flour, sifted with baking powder and salt, and beat until batter is light and smooth.

When chicken pieces are cooked, remove from the pot and keep hot.

Drop spoonfuls of the batter into the hot stock. Cover and boil over medium heat for 10 minutes.

Serve chicken on a hot platter surrounded by dumplings. Pour hot sauce over all. Garnish with chopped parsley. *Serves 6-8*.

1 5-lb. chicken
4-5 tbsp. butter or margarine
salt & pepper
1 cup cream
6 tbsp. flour
2 tbsp. grated onion

Chicken Pot Pie

Pâté au poulet

Cut chicken into pieces and sauté in the butter or margarine. Add hot water to cover, and salt and pepper. Cook until the meat comes off the bones easily.

Remove meat from the bones, pour off the stock and bring 2 cups of the bouillon to a boil. Pour in cream and gradually blend in the flour mixed with a little cold water. Add onion, salt, and pepper. Return chicken pieces to sauce.

Line a deep baking dish with pastry and pour in the chicken mixture. Cover with another layer of pastry and make an incision in the centre to let steam escape during cooking.

Bake in a 450° oven for 15 minutes, then lower the heat to 350° and continue baking for another 40 to 45 minutes. Serve immediately. *Serves 5-6*.

Roast of Pork with Garlic

Glazed Ham

Game

1 5-lb. duck
3 apples
½ tsp. salt
⅛ tsp. pepper
¼ tsp. ground cloves
¼ tsp. cinnamon
¼ tsp. nutmeg
¼ tsp. dry mustard
2 slices salt pork
1 cup apple juice
1 large onion, minced

Roast Duck

Canard rôti

Peel, quarter, and core apples.

Combine salt, pepper, cloves, cinnamon, nutmeg, and mustard. Roll pieces of apple in this mixture and put them inside the duck.

Place duck in a large heat-proof casserole with slices of salt pork on top. Add the apple juice and onion. Bake uncovered in an oven preheated to 350 or 375° for ¾ of an hour to 1 hour, or until duck is tender. Baste occasionally as it cooks. *Serves 4.*

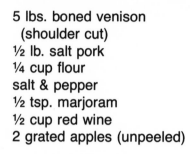

5 lbs. boned venison
  (shoulder cut)
½ lb. salt pork
¼ cup flour
salt & pepper
½ tsp. marjoram
½ cup red wine
2 grated apples (unpeeled)

Braised Venison

Chevreuil braisé

Wipe meat with a towel soaked in vinegar.

Cut half salt pork into thin slices and place them on the venison; roll and tie.

Mix flour, salt, pepper, and marjoram, and sprinkle over meat.

Melt the rest of the salt pork and brown meat in it on all sides. Add wine and apples; cover and let cook for 2 hours over moderate heat, turning from time to time while it cooks. Strain the sauce before serving. *Serves 6-8.*

2 tbsp. butter or margarine
4 onions, chopped fine
¼ cup breadcrumbs
salt & pepper
¼ tsp. savory
a pinch of thyme
1 tbsp. chopped parsley
1 partridge, cleaned
2 or 3 slices of bacon
4-5 tbsp. butter or margarine
3-4 tbsp. flour
1 small cabbage, chopped
   fine
1 large onion, chopped
1 cup water
2 or 3 slices toasted bread

Partridge with Cabbage

Perdrix au chou

Preheat the oven to 350°.

Brown onion in butter or margarine with the breadcrumbs. Add salt, pepper, savory, thyme, and parsley. Mix well. Stuff the bird with this mixture, cover with slices of bacon around partridge, and tie up with a piece of string.

Melt butter in a small roasting pan. Dust the bird with flour, place in the pan, and brown on all sides. Remove bird from the stove and put to one side.

Put cabbage and onion in the roasting pan and cook for half an hour. Return bird to the pan and add water. Cover and continue cooking in the oven for an hour or until meat is tender.

To serve, remove the string from the bird. Place toasted bread on a large platter with bird on top. Serve the sauce separately. *Serves 2*.

2 lbs. pork, cubed
2 lbs. beef, shoulder cut,
  cubed
2 rabbits
3 chicken legs
4 chicken breasts
2 tsp. salt
½ tsp. pepper
2 large onions, chopped
½ tsp. savory
4 or 5 slices of salt pork

Cipâte

Six-pâtes

Bone the chicken and rabbits, saving the bones; cut the meat into cubes.

Mix the meat, onions, salt, pepper, and savory; cover and chill for 12 hours.

To prepare the pie, fry slices of salt pork in an oven-proof casserole, then remove them. Put a layer of meat in the hot fat, pour in half the stock and cover with a layer of pastry squares, leaving a little space between them. Add a second layer of meat and pour in the rest of the stock. Cover completely with a layer of pastry, into which a couple of incisions should be cut to allow steam to escape during cooking.

Bake in an oven preheated to 400° for ¾ of an hour, then reduce the temperature to 350° and bake for another 5 hours. *Serves 14*.

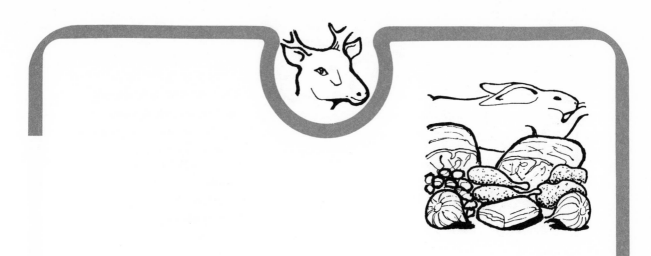

The Stock

Place chicken and rabbit bones in a saucepan. Add 1 chopped onion, salt, and pepper, and enough cold water to cover. Simmer over moderate heat for 2 hours. Strain stock and refrigerate until needed.

The Pastry

3 cups all-purpose flour
2-3 tbsp. fat
3 tsp. baking powder
½ tsp. salt
½ cup milk

Mix all ingredients thoroughly and divide the pastry into two parts. On a surface dusted lightly with flour, roll out the first half to a thickness of $\frac{1}{3}$ of an inch. Cut into 1-inch squares. Roll out the rest of the pastry and use to cover pie.

3 lbs. venison (shoulder),
  cut into 2-inch pieces
4-6 tbsp. butter or margarine
3-4 tbsp. flour
2 celery sticks, cut into
  pieces
4 carrots, sliced
salt & pepper

The Marinade

2 cups dry red wine
¼ cup cider vinegar
2 large onions, sliced
2 carrots, cut in rounds
¼ tsp. salt
⅛ tsp. pepper
1 bay leaf
2 whole cloves
1 clove garlic, crushed
¼ tsp. thyme

Venison Stew

Ragoût de chevreuil

Mix all the marinade ingredients in a large bowl. Put pieces of venison in the marinade. Cover and refrigerate for 48 hours.

Remove meat from the marinade and dry carefully. Brown meat in butter or margarine. Add flour and cook, stirring constantly, for one minute.

Pour the marinade over meat; add celery, carrots, salt, and pepper. Cover and simmer for about 2 hours. *Serves 3-4.*

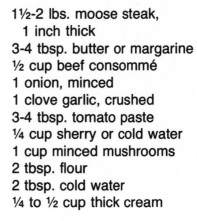

1½-2 lbs. moose steak,
  1 inch thick
3-4 tbsp. butter or margarine
½ cup beef consommé
1 onion, minced
1 clove garlic, crushed
3-4 tbsp. tomato paste
¼ cup sherry or cold water
1 cup minced mushrooms
2 tbsp. flour
2 tbsp. cold water
¼ to ½ cup thick cream

Moose Steak with Mushroom Sauce

Steak d'orignal aux champignons

Sauté both sides of steak in the butter or margarine.

Add the beef consommé, onion, garlic, tomato paste, and sherry or cold water. Cover and simmer over low heat for 1 hour or until meat is tender. Remove from the pan and keep warm.

Put mushrooms in pan with the cooking juices. Cover and cook for 1 to 2 minutes.

Thicken sauce by gradually adding the flour, mixed with the cold water. Stir constantly. Pour in cream and blend well.

Serve steak on a hot platter with mushroom sauce. *Serves 3-4.*

Eggs

6 slices side bacon
¼ cup milk
3 eggs
salt and pepper

Bacon Omelette

Omelette aux grillades de lard

Put slices of bacon in a frying pan and cover with cold water. Bring to a brisk boil, then drain off the water, and fry the bacon over moderate heat until crisp and golden.

Beat eggs with milk. Pour mixture over the bacon and cook for about 10 minutes or until omelette is golden. *Serves 2*.

3 medium potatoes
a few slices of bacon
  (side or back), cut into
  pieces
1 large onion, minced
1 clove garlic, crushed
4 eggs
2 tbsp. oil

Potato and Bacon Omelette

Omelette aux pommes de terre et au bacon

Peel potatoes, cut into thin slices, and wipe dry. Fry bacon and keep hot. Brown potatoes in the bacon fat with garlic and onion. Keep hot with bacon.

Beat eggs lightly and add bacon and potato mixture.

Heat oil in a frying pan. Pour in the omelette mixture and rock the pan back and forth slightly to ensure that the omelette spreads evenly. Cook for 5 minutes or until bottom is golden brown. Shake pan from time to time to avoid having the omelette stick to it.

When omelette is cooked, brown top by placing the pan in the oven under the broiler for 2 or 3 minutes. Slide the omelette onto a hot serving dish.

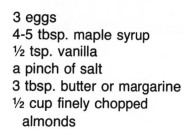

3 eggs
4-5 tbsp. maple syrup
½ tsp. vanilla
a pinch of salt
3 tbsp. butter or margarine
½ cup finely chopped
  almonds

Maple Syrup Soufflé Omelette

Omelette soufflée à l'érable

Preheat the oven to 350°.

Separate the eggs. Beat yolks until frothy, then add maple syrup, vanilla, and salt.

In another bowl, beat the egg whites until they form stiff peaks. Blend carefully into the first mixture.

Melt the butter or margarine in a large frying pan. Add almonds, pour in the egg mixture, and cook over low heat for 8 minutes. Then put the frying pan in the oven and cook for another 8 to 10 minutes.

To serve, fold the omelette in two and slide it onto a hot serving dish. Pour a little maple syrup over omelette and serve immediately. *Serves 2*.

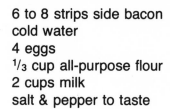

6 to 8 strips side bacon
cold water
4 eggs
$\frac{1}{3}$ cup all-purpose flour
2 cups milk
salt & pepper to taste

Bacon Crêpe

Crêpe au lard

Put the strips of bacon in a cast-iron skillet and cover with cold water. Bring to a boil and simmer for 2 minutes, then pour off the water.

Return the skillet to the stove and fry the bacon until it is golden on both sides.

Beat eggs, add flour, salt, and pepper; mix into a smooth paste. Blend in the milk. Pour this mixture over bacon and cook over medium heat for 10 minutes. Lift the edge of the crêpe to allow the uncooked part to run underneath. Cover and continue cooking for another 5 minutes. Slide onto a hot serving dish.

Serve hot with maple syrup or jam. *Serves 3-4*.

Baked Smelts

Bacon Omelette

Fish

2 lbs. smelts
½ cup milk
breadcrumbs
5-6 tbsp. melted butter
1½-2 tbsp. grated lemon peel
salt & pepper

Baked Smelts

Éperlans au four

Preheat the oven to 450°.

Gut and wash smelts, soak them in the milk, and roll in the breadcrumbs. Place in a well-greased roasting pan, pour on melted butter, and sprinkle with the lemon peel, salt, and pepper.

Bake in the oven for 10 minutes or until the flesh comes away from the spine easily. *Serves 6.*

3-4 tbsp. butter
6 slices salt pork
2 large onions, coarsely
  chopped
salt & pepper
¼ tsp. savory
2 cups beef bouillon
1 lb. carrots, sliced
1 lb. green beans, chopped
2 lbs. potatoes, cubed
1 cup tomato sauce
1 cup creamed corn
1 cup peas, drained
4 medium catfish
12 perch fillets
butter
oil

Fricassee of Perch and Catfish

Gibelotte

Brown slices of salt pork in butter, add onions and cook for 2 minutes, stirring occasionally. Add salt, pepper, savory, and beef bouillon. Bring to a boil. Then add the carrots, green beans, potatoes, and tomato sauce. Cover and cook until vegetables are tender. Add creamed corn and peas and heat for a moment.

Prepare fish while the vegetables are cooking. Cook catfish in boiling salted water. Dredge perch fillets in flour and brown in a little butter and oil. To serve, garnish each plate with the vegetable mixture and place the fish on top. *Serves 4-6*.

1 6 lb. wananish
3-4 tbsp. butter or margarine
1 medium onion, minced
2 cups mushrooms, sliced
1 cup breadcrumbs
¼ cup finely diced celery
¼ cup grated carrot
1 tsp. chopped parsley
1 clove garlic, crushed
⅓ cup 15% cream
salt & pepper
½ cup white wine

Stuffed Wananish (Fresh-Water Salmon)

Ouananiche farcie

Preheat the oven to 350°.

Gut fish, wash in cold water and dry thoroughly. Sprinkle salt and pepper on the inside and then prepare the other ingredients.

Melt butter in a frying pan and brown the onion, mushrooms, and garlic. Remove from heat and add other ingredients, except white wine. Mix well.

Stuff fish with this mixture, place on a long greased baking dish, sprinkle with white wine, and cook in the oven for 30 minutes.

Pour a little cream over the fish and serve. *Serves 8-10*.

3-4 tbsp. butter or margarine
2 tbsp. oil
1 large onion, chopped
1 15-oz. can salmon
béchamel sauce (see
  below)
2 cups mashed potatoes
2 pastry crusts (uncooked)

Preheat the oven to 400°.

Salmon Casserole

Pâté au saumon

Fry onion very lightly in the oil and butter, without browning it.

Break up salmon and mix with brine, onion, and béchamel sauce. Line a deep casserole or pie plate with pastry and pour in salmon mixture. Spread mashed potatoes over it and cover with the second pastry crust.

Make a small incision in crust to allow steam to escape and bake for 30 to 40 minutes or until the pastry is golden brown. *Serves 4-5.*

The Béchamel Sauce

3 tbsp. butter or margarine
3 tbsp. flour
1½ cups milk
salt

Melt butter in a small pan. Blend in flour and cook for 1 minute, stirring constantly. Add the milk all at once and continue cooking and stirring until the sauce becomes thick and smooth.

2 lbs. frozen cod
½ cup flour
salt & pepper
¼ tsp. paprika
⅓ cup oil

Sautéed Cod

Poissons des chenaux

Cover fish with cool water and leave to thaw completely. Then wash and dry the fish thoroughly.

Mix flour, salt, pepper, and paprika. Cover the fish with this mixture.

Heat oil in a large frying pan and sauté the fish for about 5 minutes on each side.

As the fish cooks, put to one side and keep hot. Serve with lemon wedges. *Serves 4-6.*

2 tbsp. butter or margarine
1 onion, chopped
2 cups milk
salt & pepper
3 tbsp. flour
1 15-oz. can of salmon
3 sliced hardboiled eggs

Creamed Salmon

Sauce au saumon

Melt butter or margarine in a pan and sauté the onion lightly in the butter, taking care not to brown it. Add milk, salt, and pepper, and bring to a boil on medium heat. Mix flour with a little cold water and pour slowly into hot milk. Cook, stirring constantly, until sauce thickens.

Add salmon, broken up into small pieces, and slices of hardboiled egg. Allow the mixture to warm through for a few minutes, and serve immediately. *Serves 4-6.*

Desserts

2 eggs
1 cup sugar
1 tbsp. melted butter
1 tsp. baking soda
1 cup milk
2 cups flour
½ tsp. salt
1 tsp. cream of tartar

Doughnuts

Beignes

Beat eggs with the sugar and add melted butter. Dissolve baking soda in milk and add to the first mixture. Sift flour with salt and cream of tartar and blend into the liquid. (Use only as much flour as is necessary to obtain a dough that can be worked easily.)

Roll out the dough to a thickness of $1/3$ of an inch on a surface dusted with flour and cut with a doughnut cutter. Cook in hot fat at 370-375°; turn only once during cooking.

As doughnuts are removed from the fat, place on absorbent paper, then, if desired, roll them in icing sugar. *Makes 16-20 doughnuts*.

3 or 4 apples
2 eggs
½ cup sugar
½ tsp. salt
¼ tsp. cinnamon
¼ tsp. nutmeg
4 tsp. baking powder
2 cups all-purpose flour
1 cup milk
¼ to ½ cup oil
icing sugar

Apple Fritters

Beignets aux pommes

Peel apples and remove core and seeds. Cut into ¼-inch thick slices.

Beat eggs and add sugar, salt, cinnamon, and nutmeg; mix well. Gradually blend in flour mixed with the baking powder, alternating with small amounts of milk.

Heat fat to 365 or 375°.

Dip slices of apple in the dough and brown them in the hot fat. Remove and drain on absorbent paper. Sprinkle with icing sugar. *Serves 4-6.*

Maple Sugar Treat

Beurrée de sucre d'érable

Pour very cold, fresh 35% cream over a 1-inch thick slice of bread.

Sprinkle generously with pulverized maple sugar.

Top with fresh strawberries, raspberries or blueberries, if desired.

1 cup vegetable shortening
2 cups sugar
2 eggs, beaten
4 ½ cups all-purpose flour
1 tsp. baking soda
1 tsp. salt
5 tbsp. lemon juice
2 tbsp. grated lemon peel
1 cup milk

Lemon Cookies

Biscuits au citron

Preheat the oven to 375°.

Cream shortening, gradually add sugar and beat well. Add beaten eggs.

Sift flour with baking soda and salt. Mix the juice and the lemon peel with milk.

Add dry ingredients to the first mixture, alternating with liquid. Refrigerate for 4 hours.

Roll out pastry very thinly and cut into rounds. Place on a lightly greased cookie sheet and bake for 7 to 8 minutes. *Makes 4 dozen*.

Baked Beans

Creamed Salmon

1 cup vegetable shortening
1 cup granulated sugar
1 cup molasses
3 tbsp. vinegar
1 cup all-purpose flour
2 tsp. ginger
2 tsp. baking soda
¾ cup cold, strong, black
   coffee

Gingerbread Cookies

Biscuits au gingembre

Preheat the oven to 375°.

Cream shortening, gradually add sugar, molasses, and vinegar, and beat until smooth.

Dissolve baking soda in the coffee.

Sift flour with the ginger and blend into the first mixture, alternating with the liquid.

Then add enough flour to make the dough easy to roll. Roll out the dough to a thickness of ¼ inch and cut with a cookie cutter. Place on a greased cookie sheet and bake for 5 to 6 minutes. *Makes 2 dozen.*

½ cup butter or margarine
1 cup brown sugar
1 tsp. baking soda
½ cup boiling water
2 cups all-purpose flour
2 cups oatmeal
1 cup dates
1 cup granulated sugar
1 cup cold water

Date-Filled Cookies

Biscuits aux dattes

Put the butter or margarine and brown sugar in a pan and melt on low heat, stirring occasionally. Add baking soda, mixed with the boiling water. Gradually add flour and oatmeal and mix well.

On a lightly-floured surface roll out the dough to a thickness of ¼ inch. Cut into 2½-inch rounds and place on a greased cookie sheet. Bake at 350° until golden. Meanwhile, put dates, granulated sugar, and cold water in a saucepan and cook until mixture thickens. Chill.

When the cookies are baked and have cooled off, spread the date mixture on half of them and cover with the other half.

2 cups all-purpose flour
½ tsp. salt
½ tsp. baking soda
¼ cup lard
¾ cup sour milk

Hot Biscuits

Biscuits chauds

Preheat the oven to 425°.

Sift flour, salt, and baking soda into a large bowl. Add the lard and cut it into small pieces. Pour in the sour milk and knead.

Roll out the pastry to a thickness of ½ inch on a surface lightly dusted with flour; cut into rounds.

Place the biscuits on an ungreased cookie sheet. Punch holes in the top of each biscuit with a fork and bake for 15 minutes. Serve hot. *Makes about 2 dozen*.

¾ cup vegetable shortening
¾ cup granulated sugar
1 beaten egg
1 cup molasses
4 cups all-purpose flour
1 tsp. salt
2 tsp. ginger
1 tsp. baking soda

Molasses Double-deckers

Biscuits fourrés

Preheat the oven to 350°.

Cream shortening and add sugar, egg, and molasses. Mix well.

Sift together all the dry ingredients and blend into the first mixture to obtain a pastry that will roll out easily.

Roll out pastry until it is fairly thin and cut half of it into rounds; cut the rest with a doughnut-cutter. Place on a cookie sheet and bake for 10 to 12 minutes. Then spread the icing on the biscuits and cover each one with a doughnut-shaped top. *Makes 3 dozen*.

The Icing   1½-2 tbsp. butter or margarine
2 cups icing sugar
¼ tsp. ginger
a pinch of salt
1½-2 tbsp. boiling water

Cream butter, add ½ cup of icing sugar, ginger, salt, and boiling water. Stir until the mixture is creamy.

Blend the rest of the icing sugar and enough boiling water to make the icing spread easily.

3 cups milk
½ cup sugar
a pinch of salt
3 tbsp. cornstarch
3 tbsp. cold water
1 tsp. vanilla

Blancmange

Blanc-manger

Put milk, sugar, and salt in a saucepan and heat until the sugar is completely dissolved.

Dissolve the cornstarch in cold water and add to the first mixture. Cook over low heat, stirring constantly, until the mixture begins to bubble; flavor with the vanilla.

Pour into a mold that has been rinsed in cold water and allow to set. Turn out of the mold and serve with maple syrup or strawberry jam. *Serves 4.*

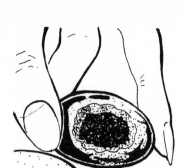

3 cups oatmeal
1 cup shredded coconut
6 tbsp. cocoa
2 cups granulated sugar
½ cup milk
1 tsp. vanilla
½ cup butter or margarine

Chocolate Patties

Bouchées au chocolat

Mix oatmeal, coconut, and cocoa in a large bowl and put to one side.

Put sugar, milk, butter, and vanilla in a small saucepan and boil for 2 minutes.

Pour over the first mixture and stir well. Spoon onto waxed paper and chill until they are to be served. *Makes 3-4 dozen*.

2 cups all-purpose flour
½ tsp. salt
1 tsp. cinnamon
4 tsp. baking powder
¼ tsp. nutmeg
2 tbsp. vegetable shortening, melted
²⁄₃ cup water
1 egg
2 tbsp. sugar
¼ cup raisins

Raisin Muffins

Brioches aux raisins

Preheat the oven to 400°.

Sift together into a large bowl the flour, salt, cinnamon, baking powder, and nutmeg. Add the melted shortening, water, and beaten egg, along with the sugar, and mix well. Fold in raisins.

Spread the dough out on a surface dusted with flour and divide into 12 pieces. After dusting your hands with flour, shape the dough into balls, place on a greased cookie sheet, and let rise for 15 minutes.

Brush a little milk on the muffins and bake for 30 minutes. A few minutes before they finish baking, sprinkle with grated maple sugar. Serve hot. *Makes 12 medium-sized muffins*.

3 eggs
1 cup sugar
1½ tsp. vanilla
½ cup milk
1 tbsp. butter or margarine
1¼ cups sifted flour
jam or jelly of your choice

Christmas Log

Bûche de Noël

Preheat the oven to 400°.

Grease a baking sheet 18 x 12 inches and line with wax paper. Beat eggs until frothy; add the sugar gradually, beating well as you do.

Heat milk with vanilla and melt butter in the mixture.

Add flour to the first mixture to make the batter, and then blend in the hot milk mixture. Spread batter evenly on baking sheet and bake in a 400° oven for 15 minutes.

Turn out onto a tea towel sprinkled with icing sugar. Remove the crusty parts, spread on jelly or jam, then roll up the cake lengthwise with the help of waxed paper and deposit on an oval platter. Decorate with icing (see below) if so desired. Chill for 15 minutes before serving.

The Icing

¼ cup butter or margarine,
  softened
2 cups icing sugar
2 tbsp. cocoa
3 tbsp. cold, strong, black coffee
½ tsp. vanilla

Cream the butter; gradually add the icing sugar mixed with the cocoa, alternating with the coffee. Flavor with vanilla.

Cover the log with the icing and make grooves in it with a fork to give it the appearance of bark. Finish decorating with holly leaves and maraschino cherries.

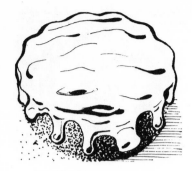

1 cup granulated sugar
3 tbsp. cornstarch
1 cup water
1 tsp. vanilla
4 cups rhubarb, cut into
 ½-inch pieces
1 cup all-purpose flour
¾ cup oatmeal
1 cup brown sugar
1 tsp. cinnamon
½ cup melted butter

Rhubarb Squares

Carrés à la rhubarbe

Preheat the oven to 350°.

Put the sugar, cornstarch, water, and vanilla in a saucepan and bring the mixture to a boil, stirring constantly. Cook until creamy. Put the rhubarb into a greased pan and pour the liquid over it.

Mix the flour, oatmeal, brown sugar, cinnamon, and melted butter; sprinkle evenly over rhubarb. Bake for 1 hour. *Makes 18-20 squares*.

1 cup butter or margarine
2 cups sugar
5 eggs
3 cups all-purpose flour
1 tsp. baking powder
½ tsp. salt
1 tsp. baking soda
½ cup orange juice
grated peel of 1 orange
¼ cup brandy or milk
1 tsp. vanilla
shelled almonds

Twelfth-Night Cake

Galette des Rois

Preheat the oven to 350°.

Grease 2 round, 9-inch pans.

Cream the butter or margarine; blend in 1 cup sugar. Add egg yolks, one by one, and beat well after each one is added. Add 1½ cup of flour, sifted with the baking powder and salt.

Mix the baking soda, orange juice and peel, brandy or milk, and vanilla. Add to the first mixture and blend in the rest of the flour.

Beat egg whites until stiff; gradually add the rest of the sugar; mix delicately into the dough and turn into the pans. Sprinkle with almonds.

Bake for 40 to 50 minutes or until the cake is cooked. Allow to cool on a cake rack.

½ cup butter or margarine
½ cup sugar
2 eggs
3 cups pastry flour
3 tsp. baking powder
1 cup maple syrup
½ cup milk

Maple Syrup Cake

Gâteau au sirop d'érable

Preheat the oven to 350°.

Grease 2 round 9-inch pans and dust with flour.

Cream butter or margarine; gradually add the sugar and beat until mixture is smooth; add eggs, one at a time, beating well after each addition.

Sift together the flour and baking powder and stir into the first mixture, alternating with the maple syrup and the milk; begin and end with the dry ingredients.

Pour the dough into the pans and bake for 35 minutes. After the cakes are removed from the oven wait 10 minutes before turning them out onto a cake rack. Frost with Maple Icing, only after they have cooled completely.

Maple Icing

6 tbsp. butter or margarine
3 cups sifted icing sugar
6 tbsp. maple syrup
1 cup walnuts, chopped

Cream the butter or margarine; gradually add the icing sugar, alternating with the maple syrup; beat until the mixture is smooth.

Ice one of the cakes and sprinkle with nuts. Place the second cake on top of the first and ice them completely. Decorate with more walnuts.

¼ cup vegetable shortening
¼ cup butter or margarine
1 cup sugar
2 eggs
1½ cups pastry flour
2 tsp. cinnamon
½ tsp. mace
½ tsp. nutmeg
¼ tsp. ground cloves
¾ cup milk
½ tsp. vanilla

Spice Cake

Gâteau aux épices

Preheat the oven to 350°.

Grease a square cake pan and dust lightly with flour. Cream the shortening and butter or margarine; gradually add sugar and beat well; add eggs, one at a time, beating well after adding each one.

Sift together dry ingredients and stir into the first mixture, alternating with milk and vanilla.

Pour the dough into the cake pan and bake for 45 to 50 minutes. Let cake sit in the pan for 5 minutes before turning it out onto a cake rack. Let it cool completely, then ice.

Icing

4 tbsp. butter or margarine
a pinch of salt
1¼ cups icing sugar
1 or 2 tbsp. hot, strong coffee
½ tsp. vanilla

Cream the butter or margarine and add the salt. Gradually mix
in the icing sugar, alternating with the coffee. Add the vanilla
and beat until the mixture reaches the right consistency.

4 eggs
1 cup sugar
1 cup sour milk
1 tsp. baking soda
1 cup molasses
4 cups all-purpose flour
1 tsp. cinnamon
1 tsp. nutmeg
½ tsp. ground cloves
½ tsp. ginger
1 cup melted butter
½ cup chopped nuts
1 cup raisins

Molasses Cake

Gâteau à la mélasse

Beat eggs with the sugar until it is completely dissolved.

Dissolve baking soda in the sour milk and add to the first mixture. Add molasses, sifted flour, and spices; then add the melted butter, nuts, raisins, and mix well.

Turn the batter into a well-greased baking pan and bake at 350° for 35-40 minutes.

Maple Sugar Treat

Molasses Cake and Oatmeal Muffins

¼ cup vegetable shortening
¾ cup granulated sugar
1 egg
½ cup milk
2 cups all-purpose flour
2 tsp. baking powder
½ tsp. salt
½ tsp. nutmeg
2 cups fresh blueberries
½ cup granulated sugar
1/3 cup all-purpose flour
½ tsp. cinnamon
4 tbsp. butter or margarine

Hot Blueberry Cake

Gâteau chaud aux bleuets

Grease a square baking pan. Preheat the oven to 375°.

Wash and drain blueberries and put to one side.

Cream shortening; blend in the sugar; add the egg and beat well.

Sift flour with baking powder, salt and nutmeg. Stir into the first mixture, alternating with the milk. Pour into the pan and then place the blueberries on top of the dough.

Mix sugar, flour, cinnamon, and butter or margarine, and layer this mixture over the blueberries.

Bake for 30 to 35 minutes. Serve hot with cream.

6 tbsp. vegetable shortening
½ cup granulated sugar
1½ cups all-purpose flour
2 tsp. baking powder
½ tsp. salt
1 cup milk
1½ to 2 cups maple syrup

Dumplings with Maple Syrup

Grands-pères au sirop d'érable

Cream shortening, gradually add granulated sugar and mix well.

Sift flour, baking powder and salt, and stir into the first mixture. Pour in the milk and mix well.

Bring the maple syrup to a boil and drop the dough by spoonfuls into the syrup. Cover and cook for 10 to 15 minutes. *Serves 6*.

2 egg whites
½ cup sugar
1 cup strawberries, crushed
   with a fork

Strawberry Mousse

Mousse aux fraises

Beat the egg whites to form stiff peaks while gradually adding the sugar.

Fold in the strawberries and continue beating until the mousse is firm.

Spoon into dessert bowls and serve. *Serves 4-6.*

2 egg whites
½ cup sugar
1 cup apple sauce

Apple Mousse

Mousse aux pommes

Beat egg whites to form stiff peaks while gradually adding the sugar.

Fold in the apple purée and beat until the mousse is firm.

Spoon into dessert bowls and serve. *Serves 4-6*.

Eggs in Maple Syrup

Oeufs dans le sirop

Pour 2 cups of maple syrup into a large frying pan and bring to a boil. Break eggs one by one over the boiling syrup and cook. Serve immediately.

Other Method: Beat the eggs as for an omelette and drop by the spoonful into the boiling syrup.

2 cups chopped dates
1½ cups boiling water
1 egg
1¼ cups granulated sugar
1 tbsp. butter or margarine
1 tsp. vanilla
2½ cups pastry flour
1 tsp. baking soda
¼ tsp. salt
1 cup chopped nuts

Date and Nut Bread Loaf

Pain aux dattes et aux noix

Preheat the oven to 350°.

Pour boiling water over the dates and allow to cool.

Beat the egg; add sugar, butter, and vanilla.

Sift flour with baking soda and salt, and mix with the egg, sugar, butter and vanilla. Add dates and nuts, and blend thoroughly.

Turn into a greased loaf pan and bake for 40 to 45 minutes or until toothpick inserted in centre comes out clean.

5 tbsp. vegetable shortening
¾ cup brown sugar
¼ cup molasses
2 eggs
½ tsp. vanilla
2 cups pastry flour
2 tsp. baking powder
½ tsp. baking soda
½ tsp. salt
¼ tsp. ginger
½ tsp. cinnamon
¼ tsp. nutmeg
¾ cup boiling water

Spice Bread

Pain d'épices

Grease a square baking pan and dust it with flour.

Preheat the oven to 325°.

Cream shortening, gradually add brown sugar and beat well. Add molasses and eggs, one at a time, beating well after each addition. Add vanilla.

Sift the dry ingredients together and gradually stir into the first mixture, alternating with the boiling water.

Turn into the pan and bake for 45 minutes.

4 eggs
1 cup milk
4 tbsp. maple syrup
several slices of bread

French Toast with Maple Syrup

Pain doré au sirop d'érable

Beat eggs for 2 or 3 minutes; add milk and maple syrup and beat until the mixture is smooth.

Soak each slice of bread thoroughly in the liquid and then brown them on both sides in a large, well-greased frying pan.

Serve with maple syrup.

2 cups all-purpose flour
¾ cup water and milk in
   equal proportions
2 tsp. baking powder
a pinch of salt
¼ cup raisins

Sugar Rolls

Petits cochons dans le sirop

Combine the flour, water and milk, baking powder, and salt; mix thoroughly.

Roll out the dough, sprinkle with raisins, and form into little rolls about 1¼ inches thick and 3 inches long.

Drop the rolls into the boiling syrup, cover and cook for 10 minutes. It is essential that the pot remain covered during cooking. *Makes 18-20 rolls*.

The Syrup   2 cups brown sugar
              2 cups water

Put the brown sugar and water in a pot and bring to a boil, stirring.

1 cup milk
1 cup oatmeal
1 beaten egg
4 tbsp. melted vegetable
  shortening
1 cup pastry flour
½ tsp. baking soda
½ cup brown sugar

Oatmeal Muffins

Petits gâteaux à l'avoine

Preheat the oven to 400°.

Pour milk over the oatmeal and leave for 1 hour. Then add the beaten egg and the melted shortening and mix well.

Sift together the flour, baking soda, and brown sugar; stir into the first mixture.

Fill muffin tins to the ²/₃ mark and bake for 30 minutes. Serve hot. *Makes 1 dozen*.

1 cup water
½ cup butter or margarine
1 cup all-purpose flour
3 eggs
1½ tbsp. sugar
¼ tsp. vanilla
peanut oil
icing sugar

Doughnut Balls

Pets de nonne

Put water and butter into a saucepan and bring to a boil. Remove from heat and add all the flour at once, stirring briskly for 2 minutes. Allow to cool.

Add the eggs one by one, beating well after each addition. Add sugar and vanilla and beat until the dough is smooth.

Heat oil to 370°, drop the dough into it by spoonfuls and cook for 5 to 6 minutes or until the balls are puffy and golden. Remove from the fat and drain on absorbent paper. Sprinkle with icing sugar or serve with a strawberry topping (see below).

To prepare the strawberry topping, gently heat together strawberry jam and lemon juice.

2 medium apples
½ cup chopped walnuts
1 egg
1 cup granulated sugar
3 tbsp. flour
1 tsp. baking powder
a pinch of salt

Apple Crisp

Pommes à la mode

Preheat the oven to 350°.

Peel apples, remove the core and seeds, cut into thin slices and place in a large bowl. Add the nuts.

Beat the egg with the sugar until the mixture becomes frothy, and pour over the apples. Sift the flour, baking powder, and salt and add to the apples.

Pour into a well greased baking dish and bake for 25 minutes or until a crispy, golden crust forms on top. Serve hot with ice cream. *Serves 4-6.*

1 egg
½ cup sugar
1 tbsp. melted butter or
   margarine
¾ cup milk
1¼ cups all-purpose flour
2 tsp. baking powder
¼ tsp. salt
½ cup raisins

Steamed Pudding

Pouding à la vapeur

Beat the egg well with the sugar and add melted butter and milk.

Sift flour with baking powder and salt; blend gradually into the first mixture; add the raisins and mix well.

Turn the batter into a greased mold, then place the mold in a pot containing hot water. Cover the pot and cook the pudding over low heat for 2 hours. *Serves 6-8*.

Serve with the following topping:
1 tbsp. butter or margarine
2 tbsp. flour
1 cup brown sugar
1½ cups boiling water
½ tsp. vanilla

Melt the butter or margarine in a small saucepan. Add the brown sugar and flour and mix well. Pour in the boiling water and cook, stirring constantly, until the mixture thickens. Remove from the heat and flavor with vanilla.

3 cups bread cubes
3 cups hot milk
1 egg, beaten
1 cup sugar
a pinch of nutmeg
¾ cup raisins

Bread Pudding

Pouding au pain

Preheat the oven to 350°.

Put the bread cubes in a large bowl, add the hot milk, and leave for 10 minutes.

Add the beaten egg, sugar, nutmeg, and raisins; mix well. Pour into a greased baking pan and cook for half an hour. *Serves 4-6*.

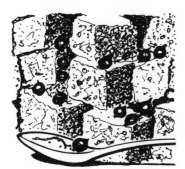

4 cups bread cubes
1 tsp. cinnamon
¼ cup granulated sugar
¾ cup melted butter or
  margarine
2 cups fresh blueberries
½ cup brown sugar

Blueberry Bread Pudding

Pouding au pain et aux bleuets

Preheat the oven to 350°.

Place bread cubes in a large bowl, add cinnamon, sugar, and melted butter or margarine, and mix well.

Combine the blueberries and the brown sugar.

Arrange alternate layers of the bread mixture and the blueberries in a baking dish, until the ingredients are all used up. Bake for 30 minutes. Serve hot. *Serves 4-6.*

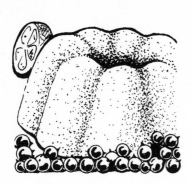

1 cup milk
the juice of 1 orange
2½ cups all-purpose flour
3 tsp. baking powder
¼ tsp. nutmeg
6 tbsp. butter or margarine
1 cup sugar
1 egg
1½ cups fresh blueberries
3 tbsp. sugar

Blueberry Pudding

Pouding aux bleuets

Preheat the oven to 375°.

Combine the milk and orange juice.

Sift together the flour, baking powder, and nutmeg.

Cream the butter or margarine, add the sugar and continue beating until the mixture is light and creamy. Add the egg and beat well.

Gradually add the flour mixture, alternating with the liquid. Beat until the batter becomes smooth.

Fold in the blueberries and turn the batter into a well-greased mold. Sprinkle with the 3 tbsp. of sugar. Bake 1 hour. *Serves 6-8.*

Homemade Doughnuts

Maple Sugar Pie, Molasses Pie and Sugar Pie

¹/₃ cup butter or margarine
¾ cup sugar
1 egg
1½ cups pastry flour
3 tsp. baking powder
a pinch of salt
1½ cups milk
4 cups fresh strawberries

Strawberry Pudding

Pouding aux framboises

Preheat the oven to 350°.

Cream the butter or margarine; gradually add ½ cup of sugar, beating until smooth and creamy. Add the egg and beat well.

Sift the flour with baking powder and salt and mix into the first mixture, alternating with the milk.

Grease a baking dish and put the strawberries in the bottom. Sprinkle with the remaining sugar. Pour the batter over the berries and bake for 1 hour.

5 tbsp. butter or margarine
1 cup chopped maple sugar
1 egg
1 cup all-purpose flour
1 tsp. baking soda
½ tsp. nutmeg
½ tsp. cinnamon
½ tsp. salt
3 cups of diced apples,
  skin on
¼ cup chopped nuts
1 tsp. lemon peel

Apple Pudding with Maple Sugar

Pouding aux pommes à l'érable

Preheat the oven to 350°.

Cream butter or margarine; add the maple sugar and egg; mix well.

Sift together the flour, baking soda, nutmeg, cinnamon, and salt and add to the first mixture.

Combine the apple, nuts, and lemon peel; add to the batter and mix well.

Place in a greased pan and bake for 40 to 45 minutes. *Serves 6-8.*

The Topping

2 cups brown sugar
1 cup water
2 tsp. butter or margarine

The Cake

2 tsp. vegetable shortening
1 egg
½ cup granulated sugar
1 cup sifted flour
⅓ cup milk
½ cup shredded coconut

Poor Man's Pudding

Pouding du chômeur

Preheat the oven to 350°.

Put the brown sugar, water, and butter in a small pot and boil for 8 to 10 minutes. Pour into a greased baking pan and put to one side.

Cream butter or margarine, gradually add the sugar, then the egg and beat well. Sift the flour and the baking powder. Add to first mixture, alternating with the milk and beat until smooth. Pour the batter into the syrup and sprinkle the coconut over the top.

Bake for 30 minutes. *Serves 6.*

1½ cups maple syrup
4 egg whites
½ cup icing sugar
2 tsp. baking powder
4 tbsp. cognac
1½ tbsp. butter or margarine

Sugar Shack Soufflé

Soufflé de la cabane à sucre

Preheat the oven to 300°.

Boil a cup of maple syrup until it loses about ¼ of its volume. Let it cool slightly.

Beat the egg whites until stiff; add the icing sugar sifted with the baking powder; carefully blend in the lukewarm syrup.

Pour a half-cup of maple syrup into a soufflé mold; add the cognac and knobs of butter; slowly pour in the egg mixture.

Place the mold in a broiling pan containing 3 inches of water and bake for 1 hour. *Serves 4-6.*

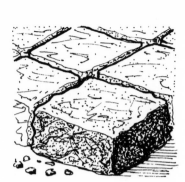

2 cups chopped maple sugar
1¼ cups 15% cream

Sugar Cream Squares

Sucre à la crème

Put the maple sugar and cream in a pan and bring to a boil; continue boiling until the thermometer registers 240°, or until the mixture forms a soft ball in cold water.

Remove from heat and allow to cool until the bottom of the pan is lukewarm.

Beat the mixture until it begins to lose its shiny appearance. Pour into a lightly greased mold and cut before the mixture has completely cooled off. *Makes 16 squares*.

3 eggs
1 cup sugar
1½ cups hot milk
⅓ cup molasses
2 cups pumpkin purée
½ tsp. nutmeg
1 uncooked pie crust

Pumpkin Pie

Tarte à la citrouille

Preheat the oven to 450°.

Beat the eggs lightly; add the sugar, milk, molasses, pumpkin purée, and nutmeg. Mix well.

Pour the mixture into the unbaked pie crust and bake for 10 minutes. Lower the oven temperature to 350° and continue cooking for another 35 to 40 minutes, or until the filling is firm.

1 cup molasses
3 cups water
1 cup brown sugar
a pinch of nutmeg
3 tbsp. cornstarch
1 pie crust, cooked
chopped nuts

Molasses Pie

Tarte à la ferlouche

Put the molasses, brown sugar, water, and nutmeg in a saucepan and bring to a rolling boil. Remove from heat and add the cornstarch dissolved in a little cold water. Return to the stove and cook over low heat, stirring constantly, until it thickens.

Let the syrup cool and pour into the cooked, chilled pie crust. Garnish with the chopped nuts.

1½ cups sugar
6 tbsp. pastry flour
4 cups raw, diced rhubarb
1½ tbsp. butter
pastry for a 2-crust
 9-inch pie

Rhubarb Pie

Tarte à la rhubarbe

Preheat the oven to 450°.

Mix the sugar and flour and sprinkle a quarter of the mixture over an uncooked pie crust. Put the rhubarb on the pie crust and sprinkle with the rest of the sugar and flour. Dot with knobs of butter and cover with the top crust.

Bake for 15 minutes at 450°. Reduce the heat to 350° and continue baking for 35 to 40 minutes more.

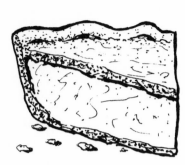

1 cup maple syrup
½ cup water
4 tbsp. cornstarch
3 tbsp. cold water
3 tbsp. butter or margarine
¼ cup of chopped nuts
2 pie crusts

Maple Syrup Pie

Tarte au sirop d'érable

Preheat the oven to 400°.

Put the maple syrup and water into a saucepan and boil for 5 minutes.

Dissolve the cornstarch in cold water and pour into the boiling syrup. Cook, stirring constantly, until the mixture becomes smooth and thick.

Remove from heat; add the butter and nuts; mix well and allow to cool. Pour into one pie crust and top with the second. Bake for about 30 minutes.

2 cups chopped maple sugar
1 cup of 35% cream
½ cup chopped nuts

Maple Sugar Pie

Tarte au sucre d'érable

Preheat the oven to 375°.

Put the maple sugar and cream in a saucepan and boil over low heat, stirring occasionally, for 15 or 20 minutes.

Remove from heat and add the chopped nuts. Allow the mixture to cool, then pour into a 9-inch pie crust.

Bake for 40 to 45 minutes.

The Pie Crust   1½ cups all-purpose flour
½ tsp. salt
½ tsp. baking powder
¼ cup butter or margarine
¼ cup vegetable shortening
2 tbsp. sugar
1 egg

Sift the flour, salt, and baking powder. Cut in the shortening, broken up into small pieces. Add the sugar and the egg and mix carefully. (If a little extra liquid is necessary, use cream.) Roll out on a surface lightly dusted with flour and press into a 9-inch pie plate.

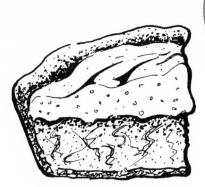

4 tbsp. butter or margarine
¾ cup brown sugar
2 cups milk
⅓ cup all-purpose flour
½ tsp. salt
2 beaten eggs
¼ tsp. vanilla
1 cooked pie crust

Sugar Pie

Tarte au sucre

Mix the butter or margarine and brown sugar in the top part of a double-boiler and melt over very low heat. Add 1⅔ cups of milk.

Dissolve the flour and salt in the rest of the milk and pour gradually into the first mixture. Continue cooking in the double-boiler for 15 minutes.

Add the beaten eggs, cook for another 2 or 3 minutes and flavor with the vanilla.

Cool and pour into a cooked pie crust. Garnish with whipped cream to which a little kirsch or rum has been added.

1 cup chopped maple sugar
½ cup chopped suet
1½ tbsp. vinegar
1 cup raisins
pastry

Suet Pie

Tarte au suif

Preheat the oven to 450°.

Put all the ingredients in a saucepan and cook over low heat, stirring, until the maple sugar and the suet have completely melted.

Pour the mixture into an uncooked pie crust and cover with criss-crossed strips of pastry.

Bake for 10 minutes at 450°, then lower the temperature to 350° and continue baking for another 30 minutes.

1¼ cups granulated sugar
1 tbsp. cornstarch
a pinch of salt
3 cups fresh sliced
  strawberries
1 tbsp. butter or margarine
pastry

Strawberry Pie

Tarte aux fraises

Preheat the oven to 450°.

Mix the sugar, cornstarch, and salt; carefully add the strawberries; place in an uncooked pie crust; dot with knobs of butter; cover with criss-crossed strips of pastry.

Bake for 10 minutes at 450°, then lower the heat to 350°. Continue baking for 30 minutes, or until the crust is golden.

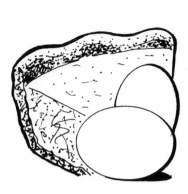

3 eggs
½ cup sugar
a pinch of nutmeg
1 tsp. vanilla
2 cups warm milk
1 uncooked pie crust

Egg Pie

Tarte aux oeufs

Preheat the oven to 450°.

Spread a little unbeaten egg white on the pie crust and cook in the oven for 1 minute. (This prevents the liquid from making the pastry soggy.)

Beat the eggs lightly; gradually add the sugar, nutmeg, and vanilla; blend in the milk little by little; pour the mixture into the piecrust.

Bake for 10 minutes at 450°, reduce the heat to 325°. Continue baking for 40 to 45 minutes, or until the filling has set (a knife-blade stuck into the centre should come out clean).

6 apples
½ cup brown sugar
¼ cup granulated sugar
1 tsp. cinnamon
¼ tsp. nutmeg
1 cup sour cream
pastry for 2 pie crusts

Apple Pie

Tarte aux pommes

Preheat the oven to 450°.

Peel the apples, remove the core and seeds, cut into slices, and place in an uncooked pie crust.

Mix the brown sugar, granulated sugar, cinnamon, and nutmeg; sprinkle over the apples. Spread the sour cream over this mixture and top with the second pie crust. Make an incision in the centre to allow the steam to escape during baking.

Bake for 15 minutes at 450°. Reduce the heat to 350° and continue baking for another 35 minutes.

1 cup maple syrup
½ cup water
1 cup raisins
1½ tbsp. cornstarch
pastry

Raisin and Maple Syrup Pie

Tarte aux raisins et au sirop d'érable

Preheat the oven to 425°.

Put the maple syrup, water, and raisins in a saucepan; add the cornstarch dissolved in a little cold water and bring the mixture to a boil. Simmer over low heat stirring constantly, until the mixture thickens. Allow to cool.

Pour the mixture into a pie crust and top with either another crust or criss-crossed strips of pastry.

Bake for 30 to 40 minutes or until the pastry is golden brown.

Miscellaneous Dishes

6 cups potatoes, cubed
1 cup butter or margarine
salt
white pepper

Potato Pie

Cipaille au beurre

Put half the potatoes and butter in a heavy 8-inch skillet. Add salt and pepper to taste and cover with squares of pastry.

Make a second layer with the rest of the ingredients, cover the skillet, and cook over low heat for ½ to ¾ of an hour. *Serves 4-6.*

The Pastry Squares 1½ cups all-purpose flour
¾ cup water and milk in equal proportions
2 tsp. baking powder
$1/8$ tsp. salt

Mix the ingredients well, roll out the dough and cut into 1-inch squares.

Note: Potato pie goes very well with fish.

1 packet of yeast
¼ cup warm water
¾ cup vegetable shortening
½ cup sugar
1 cup mashed potatoes
1 cup milk
5 cups all-purpose flour

Potato Pancakes

Galettes aux patates

Preheat the oven to 425°.

Dissolve the yeast in warm water and leave to one side.

Mix the shortening, sugar, mashed potatoes, milk, and yeast. Add the flour and mix well; the consistency should be that of a bread dough. Cover and let rise for 2 to 2½ hours.

Put the dough on a surface dusted with flour; punch the air out of it and roll to a thickness of ¼ inch. Cut into rounds.

Place on a greased cookie sheet and allow to rise to double their volume. Bake for 15 to 20 minutes.

Serve hot with butter. *Makes 3 dozen*.

3 cups buckwheat flour
2 cups water
2 cups milk
1 tsp. salt
1 tsp. baking soda

Buckwheat Pancakes

Galettes de sarrasin

Mix all the ingredients thoroughly, until the dough is smooth and even. Let stand for a few minutes, then cook on a heavy, well-greased griddle.

Serve hot with butter or molasses. *Makes 2 dozen*.

10 cups all-purpose flour
¼ cup warm milk
¾ cup warm water
3 tsp. salt
12 oz. side bacon

The Leaven

1½ cups warm water
2 tsp. sugar
1 packet of dry yeast

Bacon Bread

Pain au lard

Prepare the leaven first, mixing all ingredients well; set aside for 10 minutes.

Put the flour in a large bowl, make a well in the centre and put in the yeast, milk, water, and salt. Knead until the dough is elastic, that is, no longer sticks to the hands. Cover and leave in a warm place until it rises to twice its volume.

Knead and set aside a second time. Put the dough on a surface dusted with flour and spread it with the hands. Dice the bacon and sprinkle it on the dough. Knead it into a round shape and place in a heavy, lightly greased skillet. Cover and let rise for 1¼ hours.

Bake at 325° for 1¼ hours. Serve immediately with hot maple syrup.

Note: To serve any left-over bread, cut into slices and re-heat by steaming.

1 lb. wax beans
1½ tbsp. butter or margarine
1 chopped onion
3 tbsp. flour
2 cups milk
salt & pepper
1 tsp. tarragon
3 sliced, hardboiled eggs

Wax Bean Sauce

Sauce aux haricots jaunes

Cook the beans in salted boiling water, drain, and put to one side.

Sauté the onion lightly in the butter, without browning it. Add the flour and cook for 1 minute. Gradually pour in the milk, stirring constantly; add the salt, pepper, and tarragon. Cook until the sauce thickens slightly.

Add the beans and slices of hardboiled egg; heat through for 1 minute or 2 and serve immediately. *Serves 4-6.*

Conversion Table

FOODSTUFFS IN POWDERED FORM	IMPERIAL MEASURE	METRIC MEASURE
(flour, spices, coffee, etc.)	1 teaspoon	3 grams
	1 tablespoon	9 grams
	4 tablespoons (¼ cup)	36 grams
	8 tablespoons (½ cup)	72 grams
	16 tablespoons (1 cup)	145 grams
	½ pound	227 grams
	1 pound	454 grams
(sugar, butter, vegetables)	1 teaspoon	5 grams
	1 tablespoon	15 grams
	4 tablespoons (¼ cup)	60 grams
	8 tablespoons (½ cup)	120 grams
	16 tablespoons (1 cup)	240 grams
	1 ounce	28 grams
	1 pound (16 ounces)	454 grams
	2.2 pounds	1 kilogram
LIQUIDS	1 teaspoon	5 millilitres
	2 teaspoons	10 millilitres
	1 tablespoon	15 millilitres
	3 tablespoons + 1 tsp	50 millilitres
	6 tablespoons + 2 tsp	100 millilitres
	13 tablespoons + 1 tsp	200 millilitres
	1 cup	225 millilitres
	2 cups	450 millilitres
	4 cups	900 millilitres

Index